INHERITANCE

INHERITANCE

POEMS BY TALIA BLOCH

GOLD WAKE

TABLE OF CONTENTS

for Lorenz

_______________________________ *I*

ADVICE

Marriage is a fragile flower
that thrives on the practical:
the right amount of water,
proper sunlight, clean air,
and fertilizers in moderation.

It cannot support grand thoughts
of God or fate or the future state
of things. The weight
would surely break its thin green neck,
and the blossom would wilt, quietly.

But if, after weeks of rain
followed by unending sun,
that flower were to mushroom
into a frenzy of color and ambition,
the grass beside it would turn brown with grief

and nothing around it would survive.

LAUGHTER

Someone was laughing in your bed
laughter you could not hear
but took for happiness instead.

Beneath your feet, the stair treads shifted
as out on the harbor
a foghorn warned some distant ship.

Casually you passed through the door
and entered the room
looking for what you thought was yours.

The cool cheeks, the vivid eyes and limbs
you gathered to embrace
were grazing the heart,
the confines of a different place.

A dog on the docks gave a start,
gulls parted the humid air.
Your hands blindly sought their mark.

SHADOWROAD

We fashion the Lord in our own image.
If we are merciful and forgiving,
we say He provides rain for the crops
and looks after the destitute.
If mistrustful and careless with others,
we say He has turned his back on us.
And when we cannot find our footing
we believe
He is bereft at man's ways, or worse—condones them.

The invisible separates us.
The visible misleads.

No one may see enough to step into another's way.

I thought, *if only I could make you
believe what I know, if only . . .*

Once, when we were walking home
late at night, I thought I'd found a path
I'd never taken before,
but as we approached I saw
it was the shadow of a branch
cast across the grass
by the light of the streetlamp.

Six Years

There is no good way to say goodbye
so we decide to marry instead.
Already someone is sewing the corners
to our wedding canopy.

We have tried one last embrace at the door—
the sound of your footsteps receding
over the snow in the dark. We have tried parting
almost casually, as after lunch
on some sunny afternoon in June.

We have counted out the objects
we share and gathered them in again:
the blanket, the bowls, the oddly shaped egg cups.
Other nights, more generous,
the tears overcome us and we sit
holding hands by the light of the T.V.

Tragedy is not in the celebrated losses,
but in what we cannot lose.
Already the wine for our wedding day
lies fermenting in its cask.

Come, if we cannot agree, let us at least
be lovers no longer,
but husband and wife instead.

INTERFAITH

In choosing him
you'd wed a death
whose symbol
is the hanging Christ,

your life taken
in his name;
his death, now yours.

Like the sword
of Damocles
he hangs above you

as you stand
in the kitchen,
contemplating the children.

A Trip to Providence

Last Sunday we drove to Providence.
The winter sky lay thick about the coastal road.
Evergreen and rust everywhere nearly washed
away by gray. The cars flocked together
in an ordered silence. The stout machinery of them —
made for travel or for death. Their taillights, flat fish eyes.

We traveled to Providence. To the heart of it.
Past billboards and factories, past houses
flanked by scraps of grass. To the theater
to watch a marriage unravel before us on stage.
Sitting down, I brushed my neighbor's elbow.

I squinted at the actors hoping one would wink
at me. Or perhaps someone on the street after
as we spilled out into the dark
and walked along the new river dug out
of the concrete roads it had lain under for years.

Old capital of tolerance, costume beads, dinner forks
and knives, we saw no one we knew in Providence.
Long past midnight we returned having left nothing
of ourselves neither there nor back at home
from where we'd traveled the distance.

GRIEVANCES

The August light is dying in the trees.
The houses cast their stillness on the pavement.
The hour waits,
the hour waits upon the breeze.
Darkening, the city's stoops grow bare.
Blinds fall. The children leave.
They turn and take their voices from the air.

Generosities have all been spent.
The heat's slipped through the fingers of the day.
But we, inside,
we roamed inside and ignorant.

Bent upon the outlines of one rage,
all day I combed our grievances
so no gesture,
no gesture could free us from this cage.
Evening swallows up the windowpane.
Our minds fold. The leaves stir.
The crickets tangle with the coming rain.

Do Not Pity Me

Do not pity me my raw hands and knees
bruised from kneeling here before you,
your stride caught in my arms.

Do not pity me.
If I beg, it is because I must.

Do not pity me that what I plead
seems abhorrent in your eyes
like feeding a child poison from your lips;
nor that I have taken to a light cruelty in laughter
as one who has tasted bitter fulfillment.
Do not pity me that I have lost my way
many times, nor that I arrive wrapped in a tattered coat.

Do not pity me the way. I have traveled in search of you.

Pity me, rather, that the earth will not take form in me
as it does in others, night after night,
the houses rising again from their daily collapse.
Pity me that I am a child seated in a woman's silk —
and that the banquet has already begun.

Pity me, I tell you, for what you cannot see:
that beauty is only visible;
that there is no way to speak the serpentine paths
of the mind; that I am condemned to watch over you
so no wall, no door, no thought may ever pass between us.

FROM THE CHORUS OF RAIN AND BIRDSONG

Shall I marry you? You and almost you.
Shall I marry you, your face turned toward me
across the morning light? From the chorus
of rain and birdsong, I call your name:
you and who is perhaps you, your face
swimming up to the surface of the still-gray light,
your arms full of sleep's soft flowers.

All night I have watched your form
rising, move behind the bed, rising
to where I cannot see,
rising to take the trouble from my sleep,
the burden of my waking.

You are the hero of my waking and in my waking
I have made a dream of you, a dance of you,
you and almost you, wishing
you would be what you could not be.

Once you said, *I have suffered so much from desire.*

The white blossoms hang heavy with rain
and your eye is endlessly forgiving,
but what will you ask of me tomorrow?
What that I cannot give?

So Be It

So be it.
Here we sit
as an unknown dust settles about.
We feel its grit beneath our nails,
taste its vaguely bitter taste.

We try to place it
but can't. Still
it arrives, a companion
of a sort as we sit
immobilized.

No one calls us
but sends the dust
which arranges itself
across our room,
feeling not quite at home.

CANDLELIGHT

The flame beat against the wax shell
like the finger stroking her
now with fervor
now more gently and with ease.

Outside the snow fell softly
through the night air
covering the streets
weighing down the boughs.

And the flame beat on
like the finger
unable to reach the fullness of her pleasure

in desperate distraction
consuming wax and wick
and bringing on a darkness.

Black Moon

Black moon, black moon
that I carry in my throat
that I carry in my breath
that I don't know is there
until it comes out at night.

Black moon, black moon
burden of my life
stinging pain of my undersides,
black moon that shines on my night—
it is too hard, too hard
to wait, to constantly watch
and wonder and hope
and wish that it will appear.

Almost Married

America is a lonely place, everyone trying so very hard
to be happy, decorating their homes
with the season's latest confections.
In the short winter afternoons
we step into our cars with broad gestures
of confidence. And rush to the nearest mall.

                            Once, amid the Christmas lights,
you and I went searching for a bureau with drawers.
We considered a walnut one, then one of cherry wood.
Then you stood for a long time
in front of a slender but beautiful oak desk
with drawers and an old-fashioned roll-top.
You wanted to make of it a gift for me,
as if that could have staved off the awful truth
about our marriage.

CONVERT

A slip of the knife
to be bound to a covenant
not chosen—
tied with leather straps
to the kinks and knots
of history, Abraham's kindling
always
          somewhere nearby,
to be almost
sacrificed,
but saved by this conversion
instead.

Afterwards
she went skipping
down the hill
                    her hair
          braided
          into a thick loaf,
          deep
          blood
brown
to mother
in the house.

He's mine,
she said
and yours
as you wanted
him.

EMPTYING OUT

Let me begin again with a stone.
Let me begin again with a flower,
with a single petal, with a grain of dirt.
Let me begin again.

Let me place the stone there
and speak to it as a confidante
and ask it why.
Perhaps this time there will be an answer.

Let me take the flower and flatter it
like a young girl, as it falls to leaves.
Perhaps this time it will find a voice
and offer to explain.

SINCE YOU HAVEN'T ASKED

with apologies to Emily Dickinson

My heart sports
a modest hole—
like a plain brooch—
left by a bullet.

If you look
you can see
straight through
to the empty sky
and calm shore
on the other side.

My heart wears
a simple dress
of blue fabric
buttoned up to the neck.

It strikes
a modest pose
sticking its eyes
to the carpet,
knowing not
to ask for the sun
when only lamps
are available.

You

You breathe in, but the air is like water filling your lungs.
When you run, you are held in place by a current
as others float by in marriages and births.

You mark the hours by waiting out the day
and moving about the streets at night,
stopping in the silence streaming from other people's homes:
the orange walls, the dessert dishes left at the table,
the slight turn of the head as someone is called.

Each return home is a defeat,
yet you gather easily into your chair
and fold your hands across your chest
by the worn light of the reading lamp.

And when, someday, you are discovered,
it will be as if someone had suddenly noticed
a dark stain near the corner of the rug.

THERE WERE DAYS THEN

There were days then when we walked through the woods
to watch the leaves unfolding moist and green
as we crushed pebbles into the dirt path underfoot.

The air was acutely clear, a deep cerulean
like a child's blue balloon held on a string.
In the gardens stood those tulips with scarlet flames

jumping in the breeze, and beside them, yellow jonquils
that kept their eyes tucked beneath their hoods.
When we reached the river we sat

on the docks and watched the light drain away
from the afternoon. First the low blinding rays
across the water, and then the sky growing paler

and paler until there was just a faint smudge of violet
that deepened and spread like a bruise.
It is not that we hoped for too much,

but that we imagined so little. The wrong choices lay strewn
about like hidden ravines. How could we've known
how flimsy was what we called our home?

How much stronger the tornado of faith
that would uproot everything and throw it to the winds,
splintering the doorframes and the roof,

leaving only a vase of cut flowers
standing perfectly still on a white tablecloth
in the once dining room beneath an opened sky.

In the gloaming the river lit up with phosphorescence
as the fish came to the surface for their insect prey.
Then real darkness.

On the opposite shore lights flickered on in the factory
for the night shift. I imagine you there now.
There were days then when we were the flowers:

fragrant and soft, brilliant and brief.

II

After a Night

After a night of warm blanket and kisses,
the morning
spotted with rain and the kettle's whistle.
After the darkness,
after the arm turning like a soft shadow,
the white light
unfurls its slow unyielding weight. The walls
emerge;
the chairs hold their silence.

Along the narrow street: stained brick
and one yellow leaf
twisting itself upon the wet branch;
the empty trash can
clatters up a silver leer at the windows
gone bare.

After the encounter, the fall into the abyss:
the so unchanging sky
and the crow's flight accordioned in the glass,
black atria of the heart flapping in the wind.

Letter from Prague

after Marina Tsvetaeva

And now   I swallow   my meal
in that silence   which seeps through
emptied rooms and rattles the kitchen stove,
paints the walls a sick yellow —
and scents of you,   *Du,   Du.*

Like a wave   the silence   falls and rises
threatening to erupt from my belly.

But still   I sit and eat   fast,
to still a hunger I can only recall having had.

No more wine, no more
sliced green kiwis with black seeds
wrapped in yogurt that we shared.
No more mouths   wrapped
in conversation, warped in kisses.

Now only   this town   outside
surrounding me again. One thousand years
of history stuck to its towers.

Did I leave this water in the teapot
before I left   to visit you?
Now it swims with dust
like a faithful forgotten fish.

I sit   and eat   fast,
the chair turned half way to the door,
and wash the empty dish.

Who shall remember me now?
Even the town's many clocks are not mine.

The night streets   pull me out
damp with a March wind, dim
and filled with the movement of people,
shadows that step forward into the light
of a tram, a café, a movie house.
A town short on potatoes and bread,
feeding instead on coal and myth.

I go out   to walk   in this city
as you must too   in yours.

Yesterday   we were   two.
We forgot the hard asphalt, the blind cars,
the scrap of earth we had slipped off of.

We had somewhere to go.   Something
to do, as if there were others waiting
and the performance was ours for the taking.

Now I am like a woman   who has lost
her work at noon. Sunday night, and I walk
by the river. If not with my feet, I cross
each bridge with my eyes, but each crossing
brings me but back over another bridge.

O there, there, over the water,
O there, there, over the bridge,
I have exiled myself,
myself I have turned out the door
looking only forward, dogged by a fear of salt.

And have you counted the tears
falling   like wax
from a candle onto the red oilcloth
on your kitchen table?

But now, here, what's water into water?
This river that man has emptied,
I shall replenish. Give me one night
and   the silence.

On the train from Berlin I was still wanting
(the landscape vaguer and vaguer;
the deer coming and straining
to look at me through the window).
But now   in the wave   all
rests   at the tip   of my head,
pit of mine.

There is no bridge that can stretch
far enough across. The hole
in the ring has closed up
like a pierced earlobe healing.

TULIPS

The tulips opened
their tender red mouths.
A snow fell in.
They shut their mouths
and bowed their silky heads
to the stinging wet.

The tulips opened
their tender red mouths.
A black widow clung to their throats
spinning envy.

The tulips opened
their tender
tender red mouths.
The sun blinded in
and they gushed their dark seed.

The tulips opened
opened their tender red mouths
wide
in embrace of the sun.
She swam golden
in the center

and dropped a dark spot.
Their spines were atremble
their mouths flapped open.

The wind flew by,
rent the tender red
red mouths
and scattered them
among the many eyes.

30

MILK AND LEAD

Milk and lead follow the same lingering course
over the earth's surface—
though they never share the same bed.

The grass grows warm and sweet again
by the banks of the Spree
but you traverse Berlin's parks uneasily.

Unsure if your tongue would taste the difference—
you've had milk, but never lead—you dare not
drink, leaving it for another perhaps.

Tearing up tufts of grass, idling,
you prefer to wait for new loves to fall beside you
like fresh blossoms from the trees overhead.

Wars and history are at your back. With diligence
you try to sidestep the poison. Kisses
are just so much diversion. Lead and milk

never share the same bed, though they turn
the same dull surface to the sun.
Only in the human breast do their paths cross,
one spilling out, the other sailing in.

Another Way to Make the Argument

You will not leave your home
and come to mine.
I am a foreign land for you
with strange hours for rising
and even stranger ones for lying down—
and you travel rarely.

Once you've reached the frontier,
you cross the threshold only
with one foot, believing the other one
can rescue you once you've seen your fear.

But your other foot is lame alone.
It will leave you crawling
and that is no way to make the journey
across the river, back home.

CHARLES BRIDGE

Prague is the bridge to the other world. And on the bridge
in Prague stand three blind musicians in the February night.
They cannot see the moon's eclipse behind the slowing earth,
nor the swans below who arch their necks in darkness
and snap with stupid pride at the river broken up with ice.
Undistracted by the grieving gestures of the stone Maria
covered in coal dust and bird dung, the musicians
stand inclined like lovers lost in one desire.
The tall one holds a flute, another plays the violin
and the third, a small mahogany accordion.
As if they've heard the flutist's nod, they begin in unison,
drawing listeners, one by one, across the cobbled bridge
to stand in the gaslight's glow.

Empty rowboats rock against each other in the water
as the listeners stamp their feet against the cold
like horses whose desires have fled them.
And in the old town towers, the clocks have time
as none expected. The clocks are as dumb as the singers
are blind. Their hands perform an endless, spinning mime.

Zwischen / Between

She enters on the gray veins of a rain wind
With autumnal patience   she pares
the trivial   Stooped over the earth
in a thick harvest cloud   she crops
the fields to rust and straw   muttering
a steady stream of grief that rolls over
leather leaves   and wishes them off
of limbs sodden   Disrobed
she blows them dry   all dry   herself dry
until the earth is the last spinner
rocking   about a cooled sun
One sudden   cobalt night
she lays   her belly across the fields
burning white   with exhaustion

A train comes   hurtling down
the track bed   through the thick forest
the night   tearing the wind from east to west
heaving with one blind eye   Inside the exiles
carpet-bags heaped upon each other
move and dream and clatter in the gun-metal barrel
igniting matches trying to see   breathing out

THE SICKNESS

What we do is always already over. Like a bit of blood,
the taste of cruelty lingers in the soft cavity
                    beneath the tongue.
The moment you played with my lips—gently—
your small, moist hands wove an iron secret
                    about your fate
so that I might be racked with jealousy
for what was nothing but your loss.

Afraid that anything you found would shatter
in your grasp, you were immovable. Your words
                    were all you gave
sparingly and with cunning dazzle— each one
a ribboned invitation to a near-empty ballroom
                    that I entered gladly
and combed in vain for the one face stamped
with the dark hue of your affection.

And so, although you are just a passing interlude
to love, and I have grown tired of your pale red hair
                    and unkind eyes,
week into week I return to your room,
with its vague odor of wet sand and its not-very-clean blinds
                    drawn down to the sill.

WOMEN & WAITING SCENARIOS

I.
Work is sex and the men have it
in the next room.
I can hear the soft murmurs
held behind closed doors,
like when we heard mother and father
coughing strangely in their bed.
Frightened, we clutched our toy dogs.
Who would feed us in the morning?

II.
That stolen little teddy-bear
snatched from the store indecently
and never given a proper home
sits by the bed and cocks its head at me.
With bushy ears, a gray-furred body
and a hard nose, it probably knows
the painful charades she undergoes
each night by the flickering candlelight.
It keeps its guard for me
with incredulity, with sympathy.

III.
She has set herself in the afternoon sun
to wait and wait
to be watched
to be watched

having thoughts
about waiting
to be watched, waiting
waiting for your wafer figure to glide by.

IV.
How far away from love
is having children
and from children, love.
When I loved him
children were forbidden;
when I didn't, children
were impossible.

NIGHT OF MOURNING

Mourners in the night shake
like amphorae of wine at sea,
spilling their precious drops
beneath the pale moon.

Wandering side by side
in solitude in the night,
mourners emerge
from between the thick houses
and turn their faces
to the large, lamp-like moon —

and she is the stone
they strike with their feet
as they cross the pavement,
the stone lying cold
upon their dinner plates.

RETURN

Caught on a nail in the trunk beside your bed,
I find a long cinnamon strand of hers
the second morning back.
To this, too, I have returned.

Long nights. Icy gray dawns that drag along
the tail of history. Coal dust.
Tight-lipped shopkeepers guarding
their vegetables. Monuments. Berlin.

Once you held a sheet to my head
and declared me a beautiful bride.
We spent our nights in your kitchen
or at the theater. I searched for my past.

And now I have returned. But what of it?
Back home January is also cold, everything
driven through a soupy slush. And you are
still who you are among the uncircumcised.

Her hairs have gathered and tangled
in your drain. I find one fluttering about
in that dark, cool hole
as I stand and wash your dishes.

III

WAKING

In the morning, the world is too large
even for a king. Cities and fields
sprawled out in the sparkling sun
—and the sun a brilliant blue.

I stumble about in my confused fur
disturbed, as an animal in its cave.

Certainly there is something
I have forgotten, some thing
I have left behind in sleep, something
given to us: an order, a scent, a look
as someone turned beside the door.

In the kitchen
there is breakfast waiting:
a bowl of cereal, too sweet,
melting in milk and a coral cup of tea.

In my mind cities appear—
cities I once inhabited—gathered
in the light of their morning sun,
filled with the clamoring of children,
the scent of warm rolls
and garbage rotting in the streets;

cities that have abandoned me.

The blood comes knocking in the brain.

I touch the kitchen window for its coolness
and lay my head upon the table
in submission.

For the Generation After

Before our birth life was obscured by a dark object
like a flame hidden by an outstretched hand.
We, who adored our fathers unto emptiness,
were raised captive to our reflection in the glass.
And the image was of a barren field
when we saw ourselves; it was of our fathers'
exiled backs when we turned away.
Now, in the room, we stand before each other.

> *Between the bed and street:*
> *dust, hair, difference, fear.*
> *Between the bed and street:*
> *the floor, a dark stairwell, and a broken door.*

The tidiness of our homes filled us with unease.
At dusk the waning light visited the covered beds,
the tables, the cups in line, the objects held in place.
The dead resided there, briefly or for a time.
The dead. How many? The third secretly
charred away from our race one long night
or others who would yet lie before us in the street,
augury of our own abandonment?

> *Between the bed and street:*
> *dust, hair, difference, fear.*
> *Between the bed and street:*
> *the floor, a dark stairwell, and a broken door.*

At night our mothers wept, behind closed doors,
beside the covered beds, they wept like shattered glass.

And we lay quiet in our rooms. Across the barren fields
the hounds tore, gnawing, gnashing at the air —
baring our inheritance to the wind, snapping
beneath the window ledge. And we lay quiet beside the wall.
The curtain strained above our heads.

> *Between the bed and street:*
> *dust, hair, difference, fear.*
> *Between the bed and street:*
> *the floor, a dark stairwell, and a broken door.*

The house is empty now, inhabited by the breeze.
Barren fields have rough hands
and the curtain upon which we hoped tore in the wind.
The house is empty; still we are not forgiven.
Although we have turned away no stranger,
as it is written, still, we are not forgiven.
Now, in the room, we stand before each other.

> *Between the bed and street:*
> *dust, hair, difference, fear.*
> *Between the bed and street:*
> *the floor, a dark stairwell, and a broken door.*

Ah, Alexandra, sister, conqueror,
what rattles in your kind heart?
Nightly I hear it. No one, nothing is ours.
We offer men white shadows only —
and plead with the walls. Outside
in the garden, someone has been planting stones.
I can hear him still.

Death Valley

There is no one to lie to in the desert
              but yourself.
Swept of houses, trees, and grass,
the earth is a field of sand, bare sand
under a devastating height of cliffs
shifting with the sun in a palette of ochre,
              pinks, and blacks.

When night falls even this is lost.

A man wanders into the desert during its brief flowering
              and thinks he might build a house.
He plans to find the oasis.
Man, the keeper of lies. He wants to boast:
his oasis is filled with a turquoise shade
              and clear springs.

But his mouth is filled with sand and heat,
              his engine empty
beside the only road. And when he finally
finds his mirage, whom will he have to tell
              among the many hot rocks?

Two Women

From somewhere mistrust seeps in
like a draft under an old door. Once they were
what is called "inseparable," but then
something was said that may have been
misconstrued or she made an unintended gesture,
while speaking—but thinking entirely of something else—
and out of nowhere air rushed in. Her friend moved back.
Frantically she placed blankets at the doorsill,
but it was all too late or in vain; and the blankets
either too bulky or too threadbare.
Her friend became absorbed instead
by the deformed phantoms driven in by the wind
believing that in her cleverness she had finally found
the true face of her friend, who was stooped
below her all that time pushing hard at the threshold.

In Lisbon

Blanched by sun and salt the city lies embracing the sea,
its markets filled with oranges, cod, and bay leaves.
It is a cool city baking in a hot wind.

A city with no ends and no beginnings, only longing—
longing for a past of glory and conquest in an age
when conquest has been stripped of glory.

On warm afternoons old men gather in cafés
to eat custard tarts and sip milky coffee,
their eyes set deep into memories of travels centuries ago.

Sometimes she joins them, having come from far,
having packed her bags and casually left her country
because of a comment made by an old lover in a language

she did not fully understand, but wanted—
thinking she could belong just by pledging
some pent up emotion to the foreign streets and names.

Used Book Shop

You were so jealous
when we entered the book shop
thinking I was taking pleasure
in the memories of an old love,
but I was just at the start,
smiling at the thought
of showing you my hidden treasures.

The books flew open,
fluttered and snapped shut,
astonished and hurt
at your blind, indignant speech.

In the City

The rain has thrown its mantle over everything.
Hanging in the closet in the hall is the red shirt
we once bought together. Its left sleeve pokes out
the door left half ajar. And sitting somewhere
on your many shelves must surely be the book
I can no longer find.

I have married a different man. He lies
beside me while I listen to the rain knocking
against the windowpanes, his hand curled about
his cheek; his self curled about his sleep. Our lives
are etched into a steel engraving streaked with drops.
I turn to rouse him.

THE FLOWERS HE BROUGHT HER

Roses
like reasons
placed in a vase
slightly haphazard.
Tight red buds
that unclot
over days, unfolding
like arguments
brought to her side

for why and wherefore
as she lies in bed, wrapped
in that pale blue gown.

Each rose a reason
that falls away then
and withers
petal by petal,
as arguments abandoned
found wanting
by life or grief
leaving behind
blunt stems and thorns

like the almost child
that bled away just days ago
through the gates of horn.

First Ghosts

Bent figures. Silent. One by one, they have come
to stand among her dress-ups, dolls, and blocks.
For hours, the girl sits in her room pondering them.

When she reaches out to touch them, they recede
into the half-light, their backs rising in shame
and remorse. Theirs is the dusk of another life.

Dinner smells stream in under the girl's door
and she thinks of her mother standing at the stove
frowning over the pot. It is the hour of anticipation.

The girl sees how her mother keeps everything
folded perfectly: her dresses, the blankets for her bed,
her little socks. How can she see what lies outside?

She waits for the warm dinner while setting out
her tea set on the floor. The future does not yet exist
and the past is never explained. She picks up her doll.

THE CLOISTERS

Washington Heights, Manhattan

Brown leaves wave from the brown December ground.
Through the narrow stone slit of a window:
frost and the bird in us that shivers on a branch.
Winter travels in cars across the distant bridge—
gloved hands grip the steering wheel
and the steel girders ripple in the wind.
Waving from the river are the hands of the drowned.

September Sun

The old women in floral housecoats
who sit along the sidewalk
in lawn chairs under the September sun,
who have seen their drinking husbands
and briefcase-carrying sons brought up short
by sorrow and disease,

know
that time is not the enemy
of love, but fear,
which ties the hours into hard knots.

PROSTITUTES

On the street men were passing by
with money and bags under their eyes.

And the women
were almost leaning against a city wall.

Afterwards the women laid aside
wet towels and dirty cakes of soap

and dabbed the corners of their lips
where the lipstick had smudged.

They wrapped the fake furs and street and night
about them once again, uncertain

of how the power had eluded them. Across the way,
across from the wall, in a fifth-story window,

someone lit a lamp and sat down to a meal.
He spread a white napkin across his lap.

JUDGES

are tailors
who roll out bolts
of thought, consult
their patterns
in tattered books,
and extend their rules
across the fabric
to where opinions end,
marking off
each would-be hem
with lines like chalk.

Bent over long tables,
with heavy eyes,
they are tailors
who slice and stitch
in argument,
sewing up at last
the perfect suit—
realizing only after
that they've not
looked at the man
nor measured him.

TRAVELING OUT

Bern, Switzerland

Deep in the heart are the mountains
covered with snow, ringed with firs
and holding still lake-eyes.

Their granite rock-face is hidden
beneath coats of ice.
Their silence,
the silence of monuments.

Deep in the heart
the mountains throw their shadows.

Climbing them
takes a special expertise.

But we are unnoticing,
believing in the open sky
and the crisp air
above us—

until one day,
lost in casual chatter
we suddenly find we have traveled out

past the city, past the fields,
far past the road,
to the mountains, rising
as if there were nothing else.

LEAVING HOME

It is like slipping off a shoe at the end of the day
or taking a knife and slicing open a letter. It is biting
into the bitter rind of a sweet fruit. Mastering
for the first time how to touch a stranger's face. Or it is not,
but awakening each day from a crowded dream, alarmed
by the many rooms you've fled and the mouths
of broken teeth you've seen: surrounded by rows of beds,
valises, scattered overcoats, and cooking pots.
Trying to regard the dream just as a dream. Confused
by the naked bulb hanging overhead, casting a stark light.
Thinking that tungsten spelled backward was hope.
Going from door to door and turning the knobs,
pushing them open. Finding more rooms and more doors.

The Day after New Year's

We have abandoned all our wishes,
the ones we held onto
            into the last days of December
as our neighbors hung up pine wreathes
and cooked rich meats.

We turned to each other then
and said, surely now
            something new will come,
something pulsing and warm
like a bird with silken feathers
            that will carry away all yearning.

We look about now, still waiting.
The streets are empty except for those
            rushing off to work
or loitering by their dogs. And the tiny
Christmas lights have dulled.

A million trees have been laid to rest.
Shivering slightly, we stumble over them
            lying on the sidewalk.

THE CHINA DOLLS

Take out the China dolls, Lily,
and place them, side by side,
upon the kitchen table.
Take them out slowly,

carefully. Prop them up,
look at them and sigh.

They are a man and a woman,
looking not quite old,
but no longer young.
One of them has a broken heart.

Wherever you go,
you carry them with you. You carry them,
Lily, just to go to the corner
for some milk; you carry them.

They are your inheritance.

Winter Song

The trees are skeletons
shining in the early dusk.
The birds flock
to the crooks in their limbs,
chirping and clamoring
after the rationed light.
If we lie down now,
we just might get up again.

Acknowledgments

My gratitude to the editors at the following journals in which these poems first appeared, sometimes in slightly different versions:

The Antioch Review: "September Sun"
The New York Quarterly: "Advice"
Oberon: "Prostitutes"
Pleiades: "The China Dolls"
Poetry International: "Grievances"
The Southampton Review: "Waking"
Southeast Review: "Death Valley," "In the City"
The Southern Review: "You"
Sycamore Review: "*Zwischen* / Between"

The lines "O there, there over the water; O there, there over the bridge" in the poem "Letter from Prague" are borrowed from the Yiddish folk song, *"Oy Dortn, Dortn."*

Thank you to Nick Courtright and Kyle McCord at Gold Wake Press for giving this book a home and especially to Nick for guiding the manuscript into a book. Thank you to Lori Anderson Moseman for helping organize the initial manuscript. A special thank you to Avital Burg for her painting, *Shadow Box,* and to Katie Zoni for her input on cover design. Thanks also to friends, teachers, and colleagues along the way over the years.

Profound gratitude to Pnina Bloch, z"l and to Eric Bloch. And enormous thanks to Alexandra Bloch, Eun Kyung Min, and Lorenz Wolffers for providing support in so many ways.

About Gold Wake Press

Gold Wake Press, an independent publisher, is curated by Nick Courtright and Kyle McCord. All Gold Wake titles are available at amazon.com, barnesandnoble.com, and via order from your local bookstore. Learn more at goldwake.com.

Recent Titles:

Sarah Strickley's *Fall Together*
Andy Briseño's *Down and Out*
Eileen G'Sell's *Life After Rugby*
Erin Stalcup's *Every Living Species*
Glenn Shaheen's *Carnivalia*
Frances Cannon's *The High and Lows of Shapeshift Ma and Big-Little Frank*
Justin Bigos' *Mad River*
Kelly Magee's *The Neighborhood*
Kyle Flak's *I Am Sorry for Everything in the Whole Entire Universe*
David Wojciechowski's *Dreams I Never Told You & Letters I Never Sent*
Keith Montesano's *Housefire Elegies*
Mary Quade's *Local Extinctions*
Adam Crittenden's *Blood Eagle*
Lesley Jenike's *Holy Island*
Mary Buchinger Bodwell's *Aerialist*
Becca J. R. Lachman's *Other Acreage*
Joshua Butts' *New to the Lost Coast*
Tasha Cotter's *Some Churches*
Hannah Stephenson's *In the Kettle, the Shriek*
Nick Courtright's *Let There Be Light*
Kyle McCord's *You Are Indeed an Elk, but This Is Not the Forest You Were Born to Graze*

About Talia Bloch

Talia Bloch has published poems in *Copper Nickel, Pleiades, Prairie Schooner, The Southern Review, Tupelo Quarterly,* and elsewhere. Her essays and feature stories have appeared in *The Brooklyn Rail,* the *Forward, Tablet Magazine,* and other publications. She was awarded an Editor's Prize for Emerging Poets by *Pleiades* magazine and was a finalist for a *Tupelo Quarterly* Poetry Prize. She lives and works in New York City.

www.ingramcontent.com/pod-product-compliance
Lightning Source LLC
Chambersburg PA
CBHW032124050726
47590CB00008B/2954